MODER

Timeless Hymns

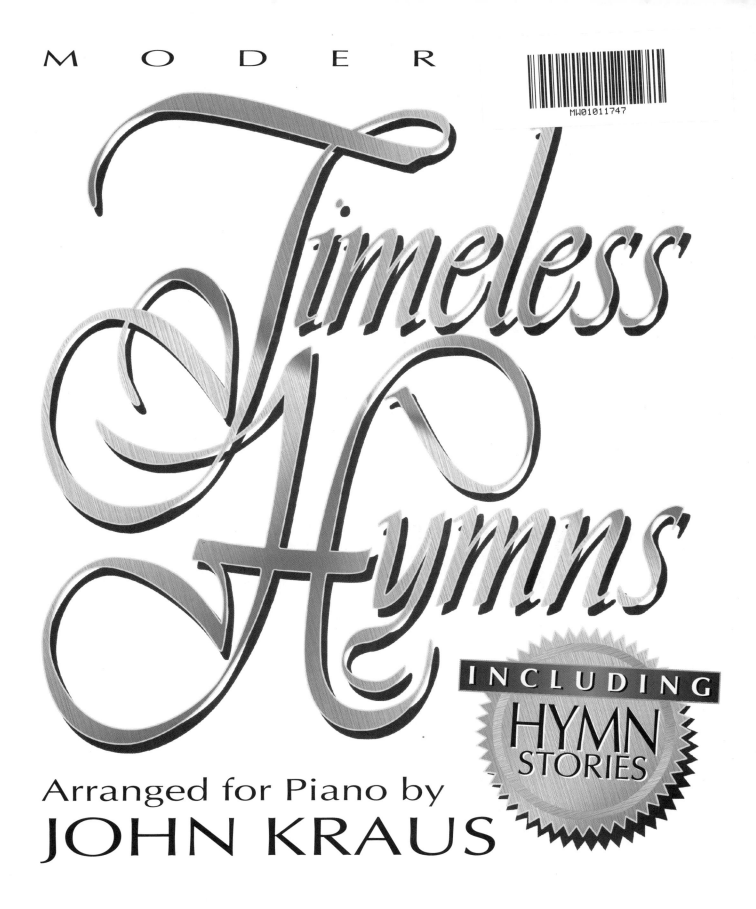

INCLUDING
HYMN STORIES

Arranged for Piano by
JOHN KRAUS

Lillenas PUBLISHING COMPANY

KANSAS CITY, MO 64141

MW01011747

CONTENTS

Joyful, Joyful, We Adore Thee

Henry van Dyke (1852-1933), the author of this hymn text, was a Presbyterian minister and professor of literature at Princeton University. In 1907, during a speaking engagement at Williams College, Williamstown, Massachusetts, Reverend van Dyke was so inspired by his view of the Berkshire Mountains that he sat down and wrote these timeless words:

> Joyful, joyful, we adore Thee,
> God of Glory, Lord of Love.
> Hearts unfold like flowers before Thee,
> Opening to the sun above.
> Melt the clouds of sin and sadness;
> Drive the dark of doubt away.
> Giver of immortal gladness,
> Fill us with the light of day.
>
> All Thy works with joy surround Thee;
> Earth and heav'n reflect Thy rays.
> Stars and angels sing around Thee—
> Center of unbroken praise.
> Field and forest, vale and mountain,
> Flowery meadow, flashing sea,
> Chanting bird and flowing fountain
> Call us to rejoice in Thee.

The Williams College president, upon seeing the newly-written text, immediately suggested that it should be sung to "Hymn to Joy," a hymn tune adapted from Beethoven's Ninth Symphony. It took Beethoven six years to compose this symphony, which fulfilled his desire to combine voices with instruments for a more thrilling and majestic expression. At the conclusion of its premier in Vienna, Austria in 1824, the soloists had to come down from the stage and turn the deaf composer around so that he could acknowledge the thunderous applause from the audience.

Joyful, Joyful, We Adore Thee

LUDWIG van BEETHOVEN
Arr. by John Kraus

6

Amazing Grace

John Newton was born in England in 1725. His mother, a godly woman, died when he was not quite seven. After a few years of formal education, Newton left school at the age of eleven and joined his father's ship to begin life as a seaman. Working his way up the ranks for the next ten years, he found himself captain of his own slave ship. On one voyage in March, 1748, he was returning to England when his ship was caught in a violent storm and it seemed all hope was lost. Newton began reading a book which he happened to have in his cabin, Thomas a Kempis' "The Imitation of Christ." The book planted seeds which led to his conversion, although he continued in the slave trade for a few more years, justifying it by trying to improve conditions for the slaves and holding worship services with his crew.

Finally, in 1750, he felt convicted of the inhumanity of slavery, and returned to England, married, and became a clerk at the Port of Liverpool. During the ensuing years, feeling a call to the ministry he began to study diligently. In 1764, at the age of 39, he was ordained by the Anglican Church and began his first pastorate at Olney. He often rented large buildings in the surrounding area, drawing large crowds with his stories of his early life and dramatic conversion. In addition, he teamed up with his neighbor William Cowper to produce an ambitious collection of hymns, the "Olney Hymnal." And to the end of his life, Newton worked with William Wilberforce and others in the crusade to abolish slavery. (Ironically, the year of Newton's death, 1807, was the year that the British parliament finally abolished slavery throughout the British empire.) Shortly before his death, Newton is quoted as saying, "My memory is nearly gone, but I remember two things: that I am a great sinner and that Christ is a great Savior!"

The tune is an early American plantation melody originally known as "Loving Lambs," first appearing in 1831 in a book entitled "The Virginia Harmony."

Amazing Grace

From "Virginia Harmony," 1831
Arr. by John Kraus

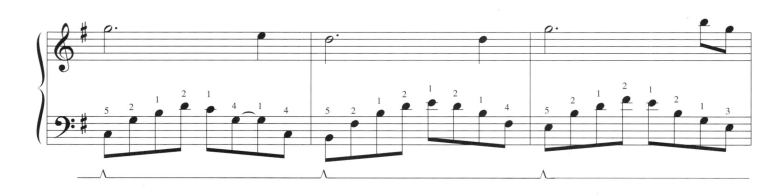

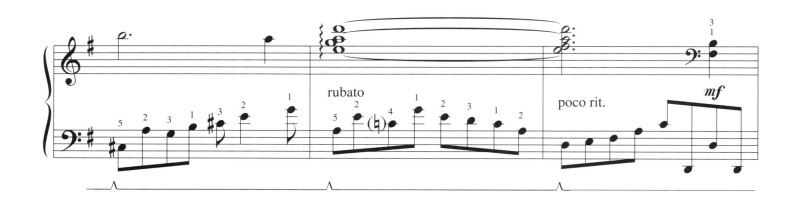

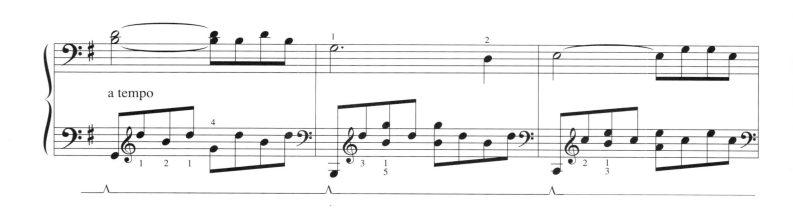

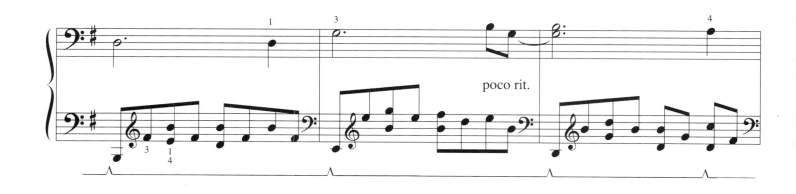

We Gather Together

Written at the end of the sixteenth century by an anonymous author, this hymn has become one of the most familiar and well-loved expressions of thanksgiving used in worship around the world.

The original Dutch text was written to celebrate victory over the Spanish overlords who had captured or exiled Holland's Protestant citizens during the years 1576-1585. The long struggle for freedom from Spanish influence is alluded to in phrases like "the wicked oppressing now cease from distressing," or "so from the beginning the fight we were winning," and "pray that Thou still our Defender will be."

The original melody was a traditional folk tune from the Netherlands. In 1877 Edward Kremser, a Viennese choral director, composer and publisher, rediscovered and published this hymn which had been largely neglected for over two centuries. Later, in 1917, Theodore Baker translated the text into English and the hymn immediately began finding enthusiastic acceptance in many major hymnals.

We gather together to ask the Lord's blessing;
He chastens and hastens His will to make known.
The wicked oppressing now cease from distressing.
Sing praises to His name; He forgets not His own.

Beside us to guide us, our God with us joining,
Ordaining, maintaining His kingdom divine;
So from the beginning the fight we were winning.
Thou, Lord, wast at our side; all glory be Thine.

We all do extol Thee, Thou Leader triumphant,
And pray that Thou still our Defender wilt be.
Let Thy congregation escape tribulation.
Thy name be ever praised! O Lord, make us free.

We Gather Together

Netherlands Folk Hymn
Arr. by John Kraus

Pastorale

When I Survey the Wondrous Cross

Isaac Watts was born on July 17, 1674 in Southampton, England. Between the ages of five and thirteen, he studied Latin, Greek, French, and Hebrew, and at a very young age began to display an ususual talent for writing poetry.

As a youth, Isaac became very concerned about the quality of congregational singing in his church. Only the Psalms were considered worthy texts: each line was read by an appointed deacon, followed by slow and ponderous droning by the congregation. On one occasion, after the young Watts had complained to his father about the dull and drab singing, his father suggested that Isaac write something better. So before the evening service a new hymn was written, and it was received by the congregation with excitement. This opened the door to more and more hymns, mainly metrical versions of the Psalms, written with a desire to "Christianize the Psalms with the New Testament message and style." Among his most famous were "Jesus Shall Reign," "O God, Our Help in Ages Past," and, what was originally a children's song— "I Sing the Mighty Power of God."

"When I Survey the Wondrous Cross," written in 1707, is a hymn which expresses the foundation of the Christian faith. It was inspired by the words of the Apostle Paul as recorded in Galatians 6:14: "God forbid that I should glory, save in the cross of our Lord Jesus Christ, by whom the world is crucified unto me, and I unto the world."

The tune known as "Hamburg" is most often wedded with this text. Lowell Mason, church musician and composer, introduced the tune in his first hymnbook, published in 1822 by the Handel and Haydn Society of Boston. It is based on a four-note Gregorian Chant.

When I survey the wondrous cross
On which the Prince of Glory died,
My richest gain I count but loss,
And pour contempt on all my pride.

When I Survey the Wondrous Cross

LOWELL MASON, based on chant
Arr. by John Kraus

20

What a Friend We Have in Jesus

Joseph Scriven (1820-1886) never intended for the words of this hymn to be published. The poem, written around 1855, was born out of his great sorrow following the death of his fiancé due to a drowning accident on the eve of their wedding day. Some years later, when Scriven himself was bedridden because of an illness, a friend who came to call on him happened to see the poem scribbled on a piece of paper lying next to the bed. Scriven, when asked by the friend how he could write such a beautiful expression of his sorrow, replied, "The Lord and I did it between us."

Somehow the poem came to the attention of Charles C. Converse (1832-1918), a lawyer, scholar and musician who was born in Warren, Massachusetts, had studied in Germany, and was acquainted with the famous composer-pianist Franz Liszt. In 1868 Converse wrote a tune for Scriven's text, and the new song was included in a small volume called "Hymns and Other Verses." Yet the hymn remained relatively obscure until Ira Sankey discovered it in 1875, just in time to make it the last inclusion in his well-known collection, "Sankey's Gospel Hymns, Number One." From there, the hymn quickly became one of the all-time favorites among Christians around the world. Indeed, missionaries confirm that it is still one of the first hymns taught to new converts, because of its profound message and appealing melody.

What a friend we have in Jesus,
All our sins and griefs to bear!
What a privilege to carry
Ev'rything to God in prayer.
O what peace we often forfeit,
O what needless pain we bear,
All because we do not carry
Ev'rything to God in prayer.

What a Friend We Have in Jesus

CHARLES C. CONVERSE
Arr. by John Kraus

Savior, Like a Shepherd Lead Us

This beautiful and peaceful tune was composed in 1859 by William B. Bradbury, a talented musician whose other well-known melodies include "Just As I Am," "Sweet Hour of Prayer," "He Leadeth Me," "The Solid Rock," and "Jesus Loves Me."

Bradbury, a protege of the gifted composer, Lowell Mason, also played an important role in inspiring and encouraging blind Fanny Crosby to use her writing talents for creating great hymns for the glory of God.

The text was a poem which had first appeared in a book called "Hymns for the Young," published in 1836 by Dorothy A. Thrupp.

Savior, like a shepherd lead us;
Much we need Thy tender care.
In Thy pleasant pastures feed us;
For our use Thy folds prepare.
Blessed Jesus, blessed Jesus!
Thou hast bought us; Thine we are.
Blessed Jesus, blessed Jesus!
Thou hast bought us; Thine we are.

Early let us seek Thy favor;
Early let us do Thy will.
Blessed Lord and only Savior,
With Thy love our beings fill.
Blessed Jesus, blessed Jesus!
Thou hast bought us; Thine we are.
Blessed Jesus, blessed Jesus!
Thou hast bought us; Thine we are.

"Sheep May Safely Graze" first appeared in Johann Sebastian Bach's "Birthday Cantata," written in 1744. There it was scored for soprano solo with two flutes and continuo (bass).

Savior, Like a Shepherd Lead Us

(In the setting of J. S. Bach's *Sheep May Safely Graze*)

WILLIAM B. BRADBURY
Arr. by John Kraus

Ped. _____

I Need Thee Every Hour

Anne Sherwood Hawks, the writer of this text, was born in 1835 in Hoosick, New York. She began writing poetry as a teenager. At the age of 22, she moved to Brooklyn, New York, where she joined the Hanson Place Baptist Church. Here she was further encouraged in her writing by her pastor, Rev. Robert Lowry.

Life was happy for Anne. She was in good health, lived in a comfortable home, and enjoyed the devotion of her husband and family. One day in June, 1872, her gratitude to God spilled out in the form of this text, which she gave to her pastor. Rev. Lowry, who wrote many hymns in his day including "Shall We Gather at the River?", set her verses to music and added a chorus. In November of that year, the new hymn was introduced at the National Baptist Sunday School Convention in Cincinnati. It was immediately popular, prompting Lowry to include it in his songbook, "Royal Diadem." Ira Sankey then incorporated it into the revival crusades of Dwight Moody across the United States and England.

Sixteen years after the writing of the hymn, in 1888, Anne's husband died, making her a widow at the age of 53. For the first time, she fully understood why the hymn had been a blessing to so many, because she herself was able to turn to her own hymn for comfort .

I need Thee ev'ry hour,
Most gracious Lord;
No tender voice like Thine
Can peace afford.

I need Thee, O I need Thee;
Ev'ry hour I need Thee!
O bless me now, my Savior,
I come to Thee.

I Need Thee Every Hour

ROBERT LOWRY
Arr. by John Kraus

Jesus, Savior, Pilot Me

This text was written by Rev. Edward Hopper (1818-1888), a modest Presbyterian minister whose last pastorate found him at the Church of the Sea and Land, located on the harbor in New York City and ministering primarily to sailors. In 1871, during his first year at this church, he wrote the poem anonymously and sent it to the "Sailors' Magazine," where it was published. A famous Philadelphia composer and publisher, John Edgar Gould, noticed the text and set it to music the night before he sailed to North Africa, where he hoped to mend his failing health. Gould then included it in a songbook entitled "Songs of Gladness" which he published shortly thereafter. The hymn found immediate acceptance, not only among men of the sea, but among all who could relate to its analogies to life in general. When it was learned in 1875 that Gould had died in Algiers, the sailors at Church of the Sea and Land mourned the death of the man who had set one of their favorite hymns to music, not realizing that their own pastor had written the words. It was not until Hopper's death in 1888 that the discovery of original manuscripts in his office revealed that he had written many hymn-poems, among them "Jesus, Savior, Pilot Me."

Jesus, Savior, pilot me
Over life's tempestuous sea.
Unknown waves before me roll,
Hiding rock and treach'rous shoal.
Chart and compass come from Thee;
Jesus, Savior, pilot me.

As a mother stills her child,
Thou canst hush the ocean wild.
Boist'rous waves obey Thy will
When Thou say'st to them, "Be still!"
Wondrous Sov'reign of the sea,
Jesus, Savior, pilot me.

Jesus, Savior, Pilot Me

JOHN E. GOULD
Arr. by John Kraus

O Jesus, So Sweet

Years ago, while listening to this song with its noble simplicity sung by one of our daughters when just a tiny girl, the arranger of this song was deeply moved to tears. What I heard was the faith of a little child as she expressed the basic gospel message and her love for the Baby Jesus.

O Jesus, so sweet, O Jesus, so mild,
O lovely Babe, Celestial Child,
Thou cam'st to us from heav'n above
To bring poor mortals God's great love.
O Jesus, so sweet, O Jesus, so mild.

O Jesus, so gentle, Jesus, so sweet,
Thy Father's task didst Thou complete.
From heaven high and kingly crown
To lowly man Thou camest down.
O Jesus, so gentle, Jesus, so sweet.

O Jesus, so gentle, Jesus, so sweet,
Thy Father's wrath for us didst meet.
For all our sins hast Thou atoned,
Thy Father's love for us hast won.
O Jesus, so gentle, Jesus, so sweet.

O Jesus, so gentle, Jesus, so sweet,
Grant that we see Thy love so great.
All that we have belongs to Thee;
Thou hast redeemed us, set us free.
O Jesus, so gentle, Jesus, so sweet.

O Jesus, So Sweet

Traditional German Chorale
Arr. by John Kraus

With tender expression